DOGS IN ART

George Garrard (1760–1826), *Portrait of a Liver and White Pointer*.

DOGS IN ART

Introduced & compiled by
CHRISTINE O'BRIEN

Picture selection by Julia Brown

STUDIO EDITIONS
LONDON

This edition published 1994 by
Studio Editions Ltd
Princess House, 50 Eastcastle Street
London, W1N 7AP, England

Printed and bound in Singapore

ISBN 1 85891 175 3

INTRODUCTION

As protectors, friends and playthings, dogs have enjoyed a relationship with humans unrivalled by any other animal. Today there are over 400 distinct breeds of domestic dog, but all have a common ancestor in the wolf, which was probably first tamed over 10,000 years ago by the Stone Age people who shared its hunting grounds.

It is hard to determine exactly how long most breeds have been in existence, though Egyptian and Assyrian artists depict dogs that can be identified with modern mastiffs and greyhounds. Most early representations of dogs show them as predatory animals, whose speed in the chase and ferocity at the kill made them ideal as companions for the huntsman and guardians of the herdsman's flocks. While the painters of the Middle Ages also succeeded in conveying the agility and grace of the hound, the dogs of medieval hunting scenes are clearly working animals.

Vittore Carpaccio (*c.* 1450/5 – 1525/6), *Vision of St Augustine.* The inclusion of the little dog adds an extremely intimate touch to the serious religious subject-matter of this painting.

In Renaissance Europe, the dog was evidently much more than a predator, and a greater variety of breeds appeared in the work of different artists. Curled up at its owner's feet both in bed and in the tomb, the dog had become a symbol of loyalty, of the continuing bond between man and animal, and even of spirituality. In Piero di Cosimo's *Death of Procris*, the dog sitting by the dead girl seems to be mourning her loss with a grief that is almost human (*see* Plate 4).

Dogs were household pets, too, as they had been since the days of the Roman Empire, and appeared in paintings of interior scenes, enjoying the delicacies of the banqueting table and the caresses of beautifully dressed women. Young men about town walked their dogs through the streets, as Carpaccio showed in his picture of Venice (*see* Plate 3). Miniature long-haired breeds, suggesting fidelity, figured in a wide range of pictures. In Carpaccio's *Vision of St Augustine*, for example, the saint's fluffy companion sits looking into space with an air of intense concentration to match that of its master; while the griffin terrier of Van Eyck's *Arnolfini Marriage* (*see* Plate 1) gazes straight at the viewer in a pose bristling with life.

Pet dogs continued to be treated as the accessories of their owners over centuries of portraiture, sometimes as pampered toys, sometimes as much-loved friends. Their presence could be used to bring vitality to otherwise static scenes and to express the status or the character of the sitter. The English painter Hogarth, whose pug Trump lived with him for many years, liked to make a joke of the close resemblance between dog and master, and included Trump in his own self-portrait as if to point this out.

In some cases pets even became the subjects of pictures in their own right. Jean-Baptiste Oudry, the eighteenth-century French artist, was particularly well-known as a specialist in animal painting of this kind (*see* Plate 11). As fashions changed, the spaniels of Stuart England gave way to poodles and Pomeranians in the eighteenth century, but the strength of the attachment between dogs and humans remained a constant theme.

Apart from such obviously cosseted animals, the working dogs of the chase still reflected the preoccupations of the country gentleman, for whom hunting was a favourite pastime. When the sporting owners of famous horses commissioned pictures of their mounts in the eighteenth century, they asked for similar posed portraits of the hounds. Ringwood, the best-known dog of his day, was recorded in this way by George Stubbs, whose powers of observation and obvious love of animals earned him a reputation as a master of such painting.

William Hogarth (1697–1764),
The Painter and his Pug.

Joshua Reynolds (1723–92),
Master Philip Yorke, later Viscount Royston.

Marie Rosa Bonheur (1822–99), *Brizo*. Bonheur was one of the
most famous animal painters of the nineteenth century.

Hunting dogs were also pictured in groups. Sometimes they appeared simply as decorative ingredients in scenes designed to emphasize the cheerful pleasures of country pursuits. In other cases they were shown in action. Edwin Landseer's picture of otter hounds (*see* Plate 17) is full of the movement and excitement of a pack in full cry. In quieter, more domestic paintings, such as John Noble's picture of bloodhounds, sporting dogs were seen at rest in kennels and outhouses.

In the nineteenth century, new technology made colour printing a comparatively cheap process. Pictures which had previously been accessible to the few could be copied and reproduced for a mass market. Animals were always a popular subject, particularly when they looked as attractive as Rosa Bonheur's sheepdog *Brizo*, a painting which combines a warm-hearted appeal with acute observation of a specific breed. Animal pictures by well-known artists were even transformed into embroidery patterns.

Dogs also began to feature in works with titles suggesting that they were capable of human thought and emotion. Among the most famous of these is Landseer's *The Old Shepherd's Chief Mourner* (*see* Plate 18). Although this picture is clearly sentimental in intention, the dog's portrait is realistic and unfussy.

The English have often been accused of an obsessive fondness for their pets. This may be unfair, but it is certainly true that British artists have always found a public ready to respond to pictures of all kinds of dog, from the playful terrier to the pedigree King Charles. For, however well-trained they appear, there is always something unpredictable about dogs. Their wild ancestry lurks not very far below the surface, and, as the last delightful picture in this book shows, when we think we are taking them for walks, they are just as likely to be taking us.

— THE —
PLATES

PLATE 1

Jan van Eyck (*fl*. 1422−41)

The Arnolfini Marriage
DETAIL

The great pleasure of a dog is that you may make a
fool of yourself with him and not only will he not
scold you, but he will make a fool of himself too.

From the *Notebooks* of
SAMUEL BUTLER (1835−1902)

PLATE 2

Traites de Fauconnerie et de Venerie (1459)
French Manuscript

The Boar Hunt

DETAIL

Nor, last, forget thy faithful dogs: but feed
With fattening whey the mastiff's generous breed,
And Spartan race, who, for the fold's relief,
Will persecute with cries the nightly thief,
Repulse the howling wolf, and hold at bay
The mountain robbers rushing to the prey.
With cries of hounds, thou mayst pursue the fear
Of flying hares, and chase the fallow deer,
Rouse from their desert dens the bristled rage
Of boars, and beamy stags in toils engage.

From *The Georgics*
VIRGIL (70–19 BC)
Trans. John Dryden (1631–1700)

PLATE 3

Vittore Carpaccio (*c.*1450/5 − 1525/6)

Arrival of the Ambassadors

DETAIL

And in that town a dog was found,
As many dogs there be,
Both mongrel, puppy, whelp, and hound,
And curs of low degree.
This dog and man at first were friends
But when a pique began,
The dog, to gain some private ends,
Went mad and bit the man.

From *The Vicar of Wakefield*
OLIVER GOLDSMITH (1730−74)

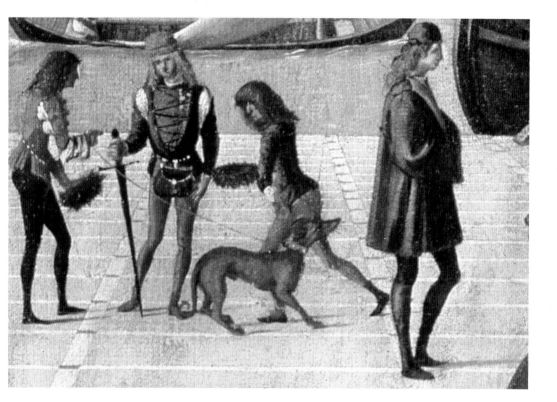

PLATE 4

Piero di Cosimo (*c.*1462 – after 1515)

Death of Procris

Poor Irus' faithful wolf-dog, here I lie,
That wont to tend my old blind master's steps,
His guide and guard; nor, while my service lasted,
Had he occasion for that staff with which
He now goes picking out his path in fear
Over the highways and crossings.

From *Epitaph on a Dog*
CHARLES LAMB (1775 – 1834)

PLATE 5

Jan Gossaert (1478 – *c*. 1533)

The Adoration of the Kings
DETAIL

All animals, except man, know that the principal
business of life is to enjoy it — and they do enjoy it as
much as man and other circumstances will allow.

From *The Way of All Flesh*
SAMUEL BUTLER (1835–1902)

PLATE 6

Anthony van Dyck (1599–1641)

James Stuart, Duke of Richmond and Lennox

You see this dog. It was but yesterday
I mused forgetful of his presence here
Till thought on thought drew downward tear on tear,
When from the pillow where wet-cheeked I lay,
A head as gairy as Faunus thrust its way
Right sudden against my face, — two golden-dear
Great eyes astonished mine, — a drooping ear
Did flap me on either cheek to dry the spray.

From *Flush or Faunus*
ELIZABETH BARRETT BROWNING (1806–61)

PLATE 7

Melchior Hondecoeter (1636−95)

Young Serving Boy and Dead Game
DETAIL

Here the rude clamour of the sportsman's joy
The gun fast-thundering and the winded horn,
Would tempt the Muse to sing the rural game, −
How, in his mid career, the spaniel, struck
Stiff by the tainted gale, with open nose
Outstretched and finely sensible, draws full,
Fearful, and cautious on the latent prey.

From *Autumn*
JAMES THOMSON (1700−48)

PLATE 8

Matthys Naiveu (1647 – *c*.1721)

Portrait of a Lady wearing a Red and White Dress
DETAIL

Not louder shrieks to pitying heav'n are cast,
When husbands, or when lap-dogs breathe their last.

From *The Rape of the Lock*
ALEXANDER POPE (1688 – 1744)

PLATE 9

Jan Wyck (1652–1700)

Pug before Dunham Massey

Pug is come! – come to fill up the void left by
false and narrow-hearted friends. I see already
that he is without envy, hatred, or malice – that
he will betray no secrets, and feel neither pain
at my success nor pleasure in my chagrin.

From a letter to John Blackwood
GEORGE ELIOT (1819–80)

John Wootton (*c.* 1682–1764)

Dancing Dogs

DETAIL

The dogs — half-a-dozen of various kinds were moving lazily in and out, or taking attitudes of brief attention — gave a vacillating preference first to one gentleman, then to the other; being dogs in such good circumstances that they could play at hunger, and liked to be served with delicacies which they declined to put into their mouths…

From *Daniel Deronda*
GEORGE ELIOT (1819–80)

PLATE 11

Jean-Baptiste Oudry (1686−1755)

The Dog

As hounds, and greyhounds, mongrels, spaniels, curs,
Shoughs, water-rugs, and demi-wolves, are clept
All by the name of dogs: the valued file
Distinguishes the swift, the slow, the subtle,
The housekeeper, the hunter, every one
According to the gift which bounteous nature
Hath in him clos'd…

From *Macbeth*
WILLIAM SHAKESPEARE (1564−1616)

PLATE 12

George Stubbs (1726–1806)

Ringwood

They're running – they're running. Go hark!
Let them run on and run till it's dark!
Well with them we are, and well with them we'll be,
While there's wind in our horses and daylight to see.
Then shog along homeward, chat over the fight,
And bear in our dreams the sweet music all night
Of – They're running – they're running,
                    Go hark!

From *The Find*
CHARLES KINGSLEY (1819–75)

PLATE 13

V Behr (18th century)

Poodle on a Cushion
DETAIL

I am his Highness's Dog at Kew;
Pray tell me, sir, whose dog are you?

On the Collar of a Dog which I gave to his Royal Highness
ALEXANDER POPE (1688–1744)

PLATE 14

Thomas Gainsborough (1727−88)

A Seated Setter

'Tis sweet to hear the watch-dog's honest bark
Bay deep-mouthed welcome as we draw near home;
'Tis sweet to know there is an eye will mark
Our coming, and look brighter when we come.

From *Don Juan*
LORD BYRON (1788−1824)

PLATE 15

Douglas Cameron (1734–1801)

Lord Grey and Henrietta Grey with their Governess

Did you ever know Yap?
The best little dog
Who e'er sat on a lap
Or barked at a frog.
His eyes were like beads,
His tail like a mop,
And it waggled as if
It never would stop.
His hair was like silk
Of the glossiest sheen,
He always ate milk,
And once the cold cream.

From *What Katy Did*
SUSAN COOLIDGE (1835–1905)

PLATE 16

Francis Sartorius (1734–1804)

Peter Beckford's Hounds

The morning wakes, the huntsman sounds,
At once rush forth the joyful hounds.
They seek the wood with eager pace,
Through bush, through brier, explore the chase.
Now scattered wide, they try the plain,
And snuff the dewy turf in vain.
What care, what industry, what pains!
What universal silence reigns.

From *The Hound and the Huntsman*
JOHN GAY (1685–1732)

PLATE 17

Edwin Landseer (1802−73)

Otter Hounds

My hounds are bred out of the Spartan kind,
So flew'd, so sanded; and their heads are hung
With ears that sweep away the morning dew;
Crook-knee'd, and dew-lapp'd like Thessalian bulls;
Slow in pursuit, but match'd in mouth like bells,
Each under each. A cry more tuneable
Was never holla'd to, nor cheer'd with horn,
In Crete, in Sparta, nor in Thessaly.

From *A Midsummer Night's Dream*
WILLIAM SHAKESPEARE (1564−1616)

PLATE 18

Edwin Landseer (1802–73)

The Old Shepherd's Chief Mourner

A man's dog stands by him in prosperity and in poverty, in health and in sickness. He will sleep on the cold ground, where the wintry wind blows and the snow drives fiercely, if only he can be near his master's side. He will kiss the hand that had no food to offer, he will lick the wounds and sores that come in encounter with the roughness of the world. He guards the sleep of his pauper master as if he were a prince. When all other friends desert, he remains.

From *Eulogy on the Dog*
GEORGE GRAHAM VEST (1830–1904)

PLATE 19

Edwin Frederick Holt (*fl.* 1850−65)

Blenheim Spaniel at Rest

I have a dog of Blenheim birth,
With fine long ears and full of mirth;
And sometimes, running o'er the plain,
He tumbles on his nose:
But quickly jumping up again,
Like lightning on he goes.

From *My Dog Dash*
JOHN RUSKIN (1819−1900)

" Blenheim Spaniel at Rest. "

F. Holt. 1871. Prize Medt RA

PLATE 20

English School (19th century)

A Sheepdog

The shutter closed, the lamp alight,
The faggot chopt and blazing bright —
The shepherd now, from labour free,
Dances his children on his knee;
While, underneath his master's seat,
The tired dog lies in slumbers sweet,
Starting and whimpering in his sleep,
Chasing still the straying sheep.

From *A Shepherd's Cottage*
JOHN CLARE (1793–1864)

PLATE 21

John Sargent Noble (1848−96)

Lazy Moments

He is very imprudent, a dog is. He never makes it his business to enquire
whether you are in the right or in the wrong, never bothers as to
whether you are going up or down upon life's ladder, never asks
whether you are rich or poor, silly or wise, sinner or saint. You are his
pal. That is enough for him, and, come luck or misfortune, good repute
or bad, honour or shame, he is going to stick to you, to comfort you,
guard you, give his life for you, if need be.

From *Idle Thoughts of an Idle Fellow*
JEROME K JEROME (1859−1927)

PLATE 22

Paul Gauguin (1848–1903)

Pastorales Tahitiennes

One of the animals which a generous and sociable man would soonest
become is a dog. A dog can have a friend, he has affections and
character, he can enjoy equally the field and the fireside, he dreams, he
caresses, he propitiates, he offends, and is pardoned, he stands by you
in adversity; he is a good fellow.

From *The Indicator*
LEIGH HUNT (1784–1859)

PLATE 23

Arthur Dodd (*fl*. 1878–90)

Hide and Seek

There is sorrow enough in the natural way
From men and from women to fill our day;
And when we are certain of sorrow in store,
Why do we always arrange for more?
Brothers and Sisters, I bid you beware
Of giving your heart to a dog to tear.

From *The Power of the Dog*
RUDYARD KIPLING (1865–1936)

PLATE 24

Alfred Duke (*fl*. 1903)

Confrontation
DETAIL

To look at Montmorency you would imagine that he was an angel sent upon the earth, for some reason withheld from mankind, in the shape of a small fox-terrier. There is a sort of Oh-what-a-wicked-world-this-is-and-how-I-wish-I-could-do-something-to-make-it-better-and-nobler expression about Montmorency that has been known to bring the tears into the eyes of pious old ladies and gentlemen.

From *Three Men in a Boat*
JEROME K JEROME (1859–1927)

PLATE 25

Ditz (*b*. 1945)

Walking the Dog

Most men harry the world for fun —
Each man seeks it a different way,
But 'of all the daft devils under the sun,
A greyhound's the daftest,' says Jorrocks J.

From *Verses on Games*
RUDYARD KIPLING (1865–1936)

PICTURE ACKNOWLEDGEMENTS

The author and publishers would like to thank the following artists, collectors, galleries and photographic libraries for permission to reproduce their illustrations:—

INTRODUCTION
Frontispiece: Roy Miles Gallery, London (Bridgeman Art Library, London)
Society S. Giorgio degli Sciavone, Venice (E. T. Archive, London)
The Tate Gallery, London
The Iveagh Bequest, Kenwood (English Heritage Photographic Library)
By permission of the Trustees of the Wallace Collection, London

PLATES
 1 The National Gallery, London
 2 Musée Condé, Chantilly (Bridgeman Art Library)
 3 Accademia, Venice (Scala, Florence)
 4 The National Gallery, London
 5 The National Gallery, London
 6 The Iveagh Bequest, Kenwood (English Heritage Photographic Library)
 7 Belton House, Lincolnshire (National Trust Photographic Library)
 8 Johnny van Haeften Gallery, London (Bridgeman Art Library)
 9 Dunham Massey, Cheshire (National Trust Photographic Library)
10 Wallington, Northumberland (National Trust Photographic Library)
11 The Burrell Collection, Glasgow
12 Private Collection (Bridgeman Art Library)
13 Rafael Vals Gallery, London (Bridgeman Art Library)
14 Petworth House, Sussex (National Trust Photographic Library)
15 Dunham Massey, Cheshire (National Trust Photographic Library)
16 Bearstead Collection, Upton House, Warwickshire (National Trust Photographic Library)
17 Roy Miles Gallery, London (Bridgeman Art Library)
18 Courtesy of the Board of Trustees of the Victoria & Albert Museum, London (Bridgeman Art Library)
19 Bonham's, London (Bridgeman Art Library)
20 Bonham's, London (Bridgeman Art Library)
21 & Cover (detail) City Art Gallery, Leeds (Bridgeman Art Library)
22 The Hermitage, St Petersburg (Bridgeman Art Library)
23 Bonham's, London (Bridgeman Art Library)
24 Private Collection (Bridgeman Art Library)
25 Private Collection (Bridgeman Art Library) © The Artist